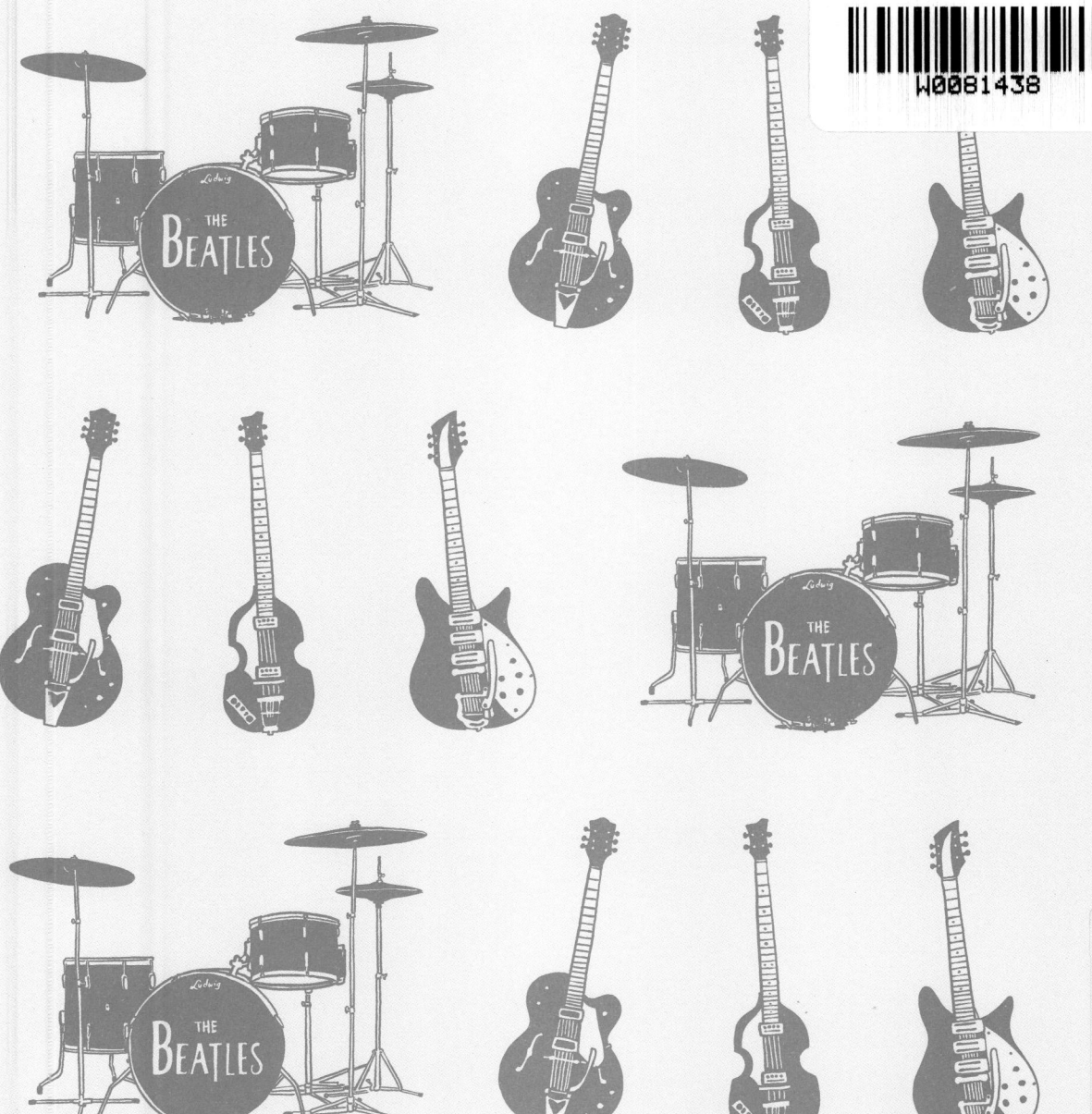

We are The Beatles

THE Beatles

Ludwig

BRAD MELTZER

illustrated by Christopher Eliopoulos

ROCKY POND BOOKS

I'm Paul McCartney.
One of my earliest memories is of lying on the floor and listening to my dad play piano.

LEARN TO PLAY PIANO, AND YOU'LL GET INVITED TO PARTIES.

I didn't take fancy lessons—I learned by ear, just like him.

I am John Lennon.
When I was five, I went to live with my aunt and got my first musical instrument, a harmonica.

IF YOU CAN PLAY IT BY TOMORROW MORNING, JOHN, IT'S YOURS.

YOU GOT IT.

AUNT MIMI

My aunt made me wait until Christmas, but getting that harmonica was one of the great moments of my life.

I grew up in Liverpool, England. It was a hardworking place. We didn't have much money, but it was home.

C'MON, PAUL. YOU'RE LATE FOR THE BARBER.

WHAT BARBER?

THE ONE WE ALWAYS GO TO... ON PENNY LANE.

THAT SEEMS LIKE IT'LL BE IMPORTANT LATER.

Liverpool was a city with lots to explore. I loved investigating these grounds not far from where I grew up.

WHAT'S THIS PLACE CALLED AGAIN?

STRAWBERRY FIELD.

NOW, SHHHH, LET'S GO...

I FEEL LIKE THAT'S GOING TO BE IMPORTANT TOO.

One of the best parts of Liverpool was it had so many great music stores, packed with interesting new bands and songs from America. That gave me what I loved most...

New music.

When I heard the song "Rock Around the Clock," I felt a tingle up my spine.

They even had a new term for it: rock and roll.

ONE, TWO, THREE O'CLOCK, FOUR O'CLOCK,

ROCK...

THE U.K.'S FIRST #1 ROCK AND ROLL SONG
BILL HALEY AND HIS COMETS - 1955

I loved Little Richard, and I'll never forget the first time I heard Elvis Presley sing "Heartbreak Hotel."

My whole life changed from then on.

JOHN, WHAT IS THAT NOISE?!

THIS IS IT!

THIS IS WHAT I NEED TO DO!

I wanted to make music.
For my fourteenth birthday, my dad got me a used trumpet.

I started on the harmonica, but eventually switched to the guitar, since it was way more rock and roll.
I started dressing the part too.

JOHN, YOU'RE PUTTING VASELINE IN YOUR HAIR?

TRUST ME, IT'S COOL.

When I was fourteen, my mother died from breast cancer. For me, music is more than just something you listen to. In those moments when you're down, the right song can lift you and make you forget about the pain.

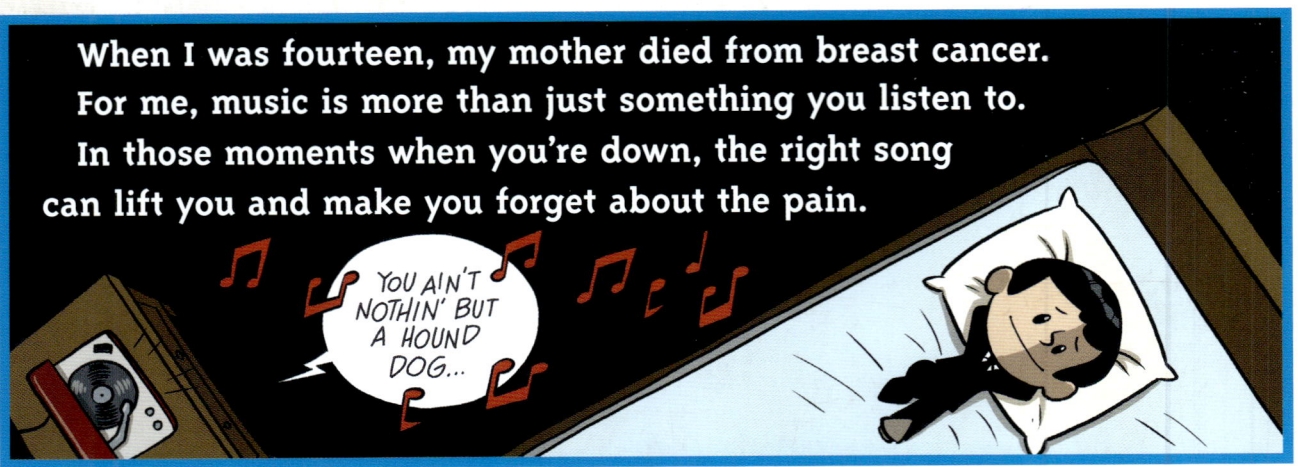

New friends.

I am George Harrison.
I also grew up in Liverpool, though my favorite parts were out in nature, walking along the mud cliffs and through the woods.

One day, I heard Elvis singing "Heartbreak Hotel." It changed the course of my life.

...DOWN AT THE END OF LONELY STREET...

Soon, I became obsessed with guitars.

I'd daydream about guitars. In school, I'd draw them.

YOU REALLY LOVE GUITARS, DON'T YOU, GEORGE?

I even tried making my own guitar, but once as I overtightened the strings...

SNAP!

Eventually, my mum bought me my own guitar.
She'd stay up until three in the morning, sipping tea and cheering me on.
She knew nothing made me happier than creating music.

Paul met John when Paul was fifteen and John was seventeen. He was with his band, playing the song "Come Go with Me," but since he didn't know the words, he made up his own...

Backstage, John liked the fact that Paul knew all the words to...

Paul was as good a musician as John was—and could play even better. John had to ask himself the question:

Was it more important to be a great individual, or to make the group the best it could be?

Even back then, we knew that making rock and roll wasn't easy.
It takes hard work.
This is how we practiced.

He was my mirror.

My model.

My equal.

At the start, it went pretty poorly.
This was the moment I was supposed to play my first solo.
I was so nervous and scared.

I couldn't.
I felt everyone staring at me.

After the show, I told John I couldn't be the lead guitarist.
We still needed someone to play lead.
But I had an idea.

George could most certainly play.
He knew more chords and made us better guitar players.

Now all we needed was a proper name.
For a while, we were Johnny and the Moondogs.

He was right. We were crummy, terrible, an embarrassment.

Over time, we added a drummer and a few different members.

The sound didn't get much better.

Soon, people stopped hiring us.

Even our families started to worry.

Eventually, we got an offer to play in Hamburg, Germany.

The club was filthy, and the housing was so bad, you could smell the toilets.

But it gave us experience.

During multiple trips and thirty-eight weeks, we played over 1,100 hours.

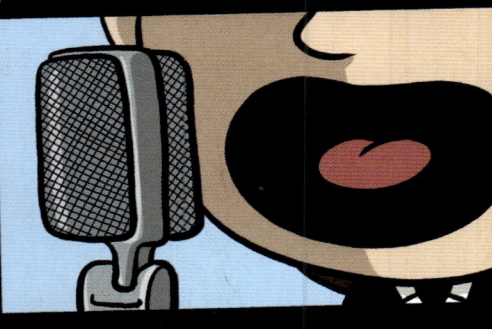

That's three hours every night for almost a year.

We arrived there as boys...

When we got back to Liverpool,
for the first time, we were really cheered.

From there, we got some professional help.

Then we got new outfits...

and a brilliant recording studio.

There was only one thing missing.

I am Ringo Starr.

I grew up in one of the roughest neighborhoods in Liverpool.

I was sick a lot as a kid and spent almost two years in the hospital.

I'd stare out the window, just wishing for someone to play with.

At eight years old, I heard Gene Autry singing "South of the Border."

When I was little, my family gave me different instruments.

But my favorite was the drums.

We didn't have much money, so I made my own set from biscuit tins.

I didn't even have proper drumsticks.

For years, I practiced and played with other bands.

Then one morning, The Beatles' manager came to my house.

Once Ringo was with us, the band felt complete.

Back then, what set us apart was that we wrote our own songs. Songwriting isn't easy.

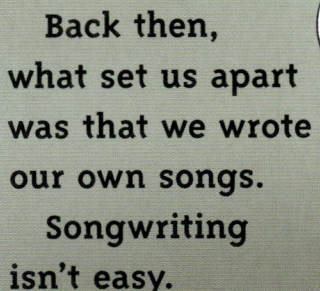

THIS ONE'S CALLED "LOVE ME DO."

I DO LIKE IT, BUT IT COULD USE SOME HARMONICA.

OH, A HARMONICA WOULD BE BRILLIANT.

We wrote music the same way we used to practice guitar: eyeball to eyeball.

Writing a great song requires patience and perseverance.

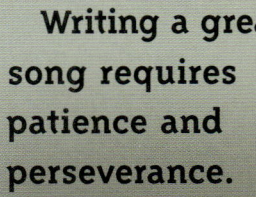

INSTEAD OF SHE LOVES YOU YEAH, YEAH, YEAH... WHAT ABOUT THE MORE PROPER YES, YES, YES?

DAD, THAT'S TERRIBLE.

The first draft you write isn't usually the best draft.

THIS ONE'S CALLED "PLEASE PLEASE ME."

CAN YOU MAKE IT FASTER?

OH THAT'S ALL RIGHT, YES.

When we were done recording, they told us...

GENTLEMEN, YOU'VE JUST MADE YOUR FIRST NUMBER ONE RECORD.

All we had to do now was convince...

The rest of the world.
In America, our first three singles flopped.
Then the fourth one came out.

LADIES AND GENTLEMEN...
THE BEATLES...

LET'S BRING THEM OUT.

It was called...

I WANT TO HOLD YOUR HAAAAAND...

I WANT TO HOLD YOUR HAAAAAND...

Sunday night, February 9, 1964, we played live on *The Ed Sullivan Show*.
Seventy-three million people were watching.
Elvis himself sent us a telegram.
From there...

It was Beatlemania.

The more we played together...

the bigger we got...

and made movies.

Even cartoons.

But what made us The Beatles were the songs, and how well we worked together.

Over time, we experimented with new sounds that mixed folk, blues, and all the other music we loved growing up...

and the more we evolved and advanced.

We tried on new styles. . .

One of us would have an idea. . .

then we'd go back and forth until it was done.

and we traveled the world, perfecting our skills on groovy new instruments.

But we never forgot where we came from.

Most of all, we challenged ourselves. . .

and pushed boundaries.

But want to know the real secret of The Beatles?

Each of us made the others better.

As the band got more popular, our ideas got bigger.

FOR THE COVER OF THE NEW ALBUM, LET'S SHOW A BUNCH OF PEOPLE WE ADMIRE!

EINSTEIN!

LAUREL AND HARDY!

LEWIS CARROLL!

IT'LL BE A BIG COLLAGE. SOMETHING YOU CAN LOOK AT AND STUDY FOR YEARS.

We went to the local costume shop.

EVERYONE PICK A COLOR...

The result was music history.

SGT. PEPPER'S LONELY HEARTS CLUB BAND – 1967

We wrote songs for good times...

and songs for tough times.

Of course, some songs took on a life of their own.
One day, I woke up with a tune in my head.

John and I worked on it for weeks.

Our last live gig together was on a rooftop in central London.

For the album, I had the idea for the title song after a dream about my mother. In the dream, she told me, "It will be all right, just let it be."

In our lives, we were working-class teenagers.
We didn't go to fancy schools,
   or get expensive lessons.
But we found what we loved:
Making music with our best mates.

Life isn't meant to be lived alone.

Here's our secret:

Find what you love—and find friends who love it just as much.

Laugh together.

Dream together.

Create together.

Make each other better.

When it gets hard, you'll be able to get by...

Individually, we are one note.
Together, little darling, we are a song.
There are four of us, but really one of us,
all our hearts beating at the same time.

The best music is the music you make together.
And the essential message will never change: Love.
It really is all you need.

We are The Beatles.
Come together.

"And in the end, the love you take is equal to the love you make."
—The Beatles

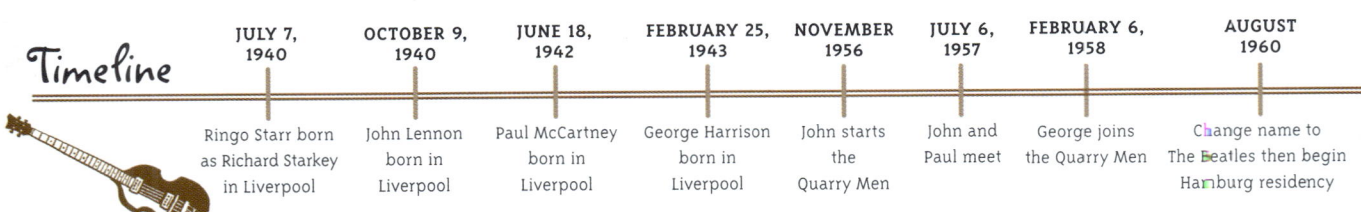

Timeline

JULY 7, 1940	OCTOBER 9, 1940	JUNE 18, 1942	FEBRUARY 25, 1943	NOVEMBER 1956	JULY 6, 1957	FEBRUARY 6, 1958	AUGUST 1960
Ringo Starr born as Richard Starkey in Liverpool	John Lennon born in Liverpool	Paul McCartney born in Liverpool	George Harrison born in Liverpool	John starts the Quarry Men	John and Paul meet	George joins the Quarry Men	Change name to The Beatles then begin Hamburg residency

Paul and John, 1962

Rooftop concert, 1969

DECEMBER 1961	AUGUST 1962	OCTOBER 5, 1962	FEBRUARY 9, 1964	APRIL 1970	DECEMBER 8, 1980	1988	NOVEMBER 29, 2001
Brian Epstein becomes manager	Ringo joins The Beatles	"Love Me Do" debuts	Play live on *The Ed Sullivan Show*	The Beatles break up	John Lennon killed in New York City	Inducted into the Rock & Roll Hall of Fame	George Harrison dies in Los Angeles from lung cancer

For Matt Oshinsky, Adam Flam, and Bobby-boy,
who brought The Beatles into my life
—B.M.

For Clayton Cowles, a fab human and,
if possible, a bigger Beatles fan than me
—C.E.

For historical accuracy, we used the Beatles' actual words whenever possible. For more of their true voices, we recommend and acknowledge the below works. Special thanks to the incredible Mark Lewisohn for his input on early drafts.

···

SOURCES

The Beatles Anthology by The Beatles (Chronicle Books, 2000)

Tune In: The Beatles: All These Years, by Mark Lewisohn (Crown Archetype, 2013)

Paul McCartney: Many Years from Now by Barry Miles (Henry Holt, 1998)

Love Me Do! The Beatles' Progress by Michael Braun (Graymalkin Media, 2019)

John Lennon: The Life by Philip Norman (Ecco, 2009)

The Fifth Beatle: The Brian Epstein Story by Vivek J. Tiwary, illustrated by Andrew C. Robinson with Kyle Baker, contributions by Steve Dutro (M Press, 2023)

The Beatles: Get Back documentary, directed and produced by Peter Jackson (2021)

FURTHER READING AND VIEWING FOR KIDS

Who Were The Beatles? by Geoff Edgers (Penguin Workshop, 2006)

What Is Rock and Roll? by Jim O'Connor (Penguin Workshop, 2017)

Imagine by John Lennon and illustrated by Jean Jullien (Clarion, 2017)

Yellow Submarine movie, directed by George Dunning (1968)

···

ROCKY POND BOOKS
An imprint of Penguin Random House LLC • 1745 Broadway, New York, New York 10019

First published in the United States of America by Rocky Pond Books, an imprint of Penguin Random House LLC, 2025

Text copyright © 2025 by Forty-four Steps, Inc.
Illustrations copyright © 2025 by Christopher Eliopoulos • Coloring by K.J. Díaz with Christopher Eliopoulos

Visit us online at PenguinRandomHouse.com.

Library of Congress Cataloging-in-Publication Data is available.

Photo on page 38 courtesy of Globe Photos; photo on rooftop courtesy of Dom Slike / Alamy Stock Photo;
photo of John and Paul with guitars ("My dad told Paul that John was trouble, but he turned out to be my brother's best friend") courtesy of and © Mike McCartney.

Manufactured in China • ISBN 9780593533451 • 10 9 8 7 6 5 4 3 2 1

TOPL

Design by Jason Henry • Text set in Triplex • The illustrator created the artwork for this book using Wacom Cintiq and Clip Studio Paint with custom pencils and brushes.